Dark Matters
Poems of Intentional Artistry

Laura Kester Duerrwaechter

Original Art by Nicolaus Seegel

Copyright

ISBN: Authortunities Press 978-1-959048-32-9
First Edition

Interior Layout and Design: Laura Kester Duerrwaechter
Cover and interior art: Nicolaus Seegel

Published in the United States of America
Books available on Amazon.com

Preface

The decision to republish this themed poetry collection emerged from a moment of personal rediscovery. I rarely revisit my own poetry, but this selection delves into a darker spectrum, capturing insightful moments along a journey toward Yin and Yang.

Art supporting art - the original artwork was created by Nicolaus, a young artist whose life experiences vastly differ from my own. His paintings build bridges to my words, fostering mutual respect between artist and author. Given free rein to interpret the poems, Nicolaus's artwork draws readers deeper into a brilliant mind that has traveled into darkness and emerged transformed. The collection's format honors the ancient Greek poetic tradition of Reverse Ekphrasis.
—Laura

Table of Contents

ABIDING FLEDGLING

It is time
to leave
the nest of my dreams.
Or
I shall perish
in the tall pines,
where the air is thin.

Arthritis creeps.
Aging feathers –
barbs and veins
exposed.

Rock slides.
Talons unsteady.
Destiny.

Virgin flight,
solitary and leaving.
Plunging spiral
on an unforgiving current.
Plummet and final breath.

Wind shifts -
Rebirth
Unwelcome.

Journey unbroken –
pieces scattered.
My life
unrecognizable
in sedimentary
layers upon the ground.

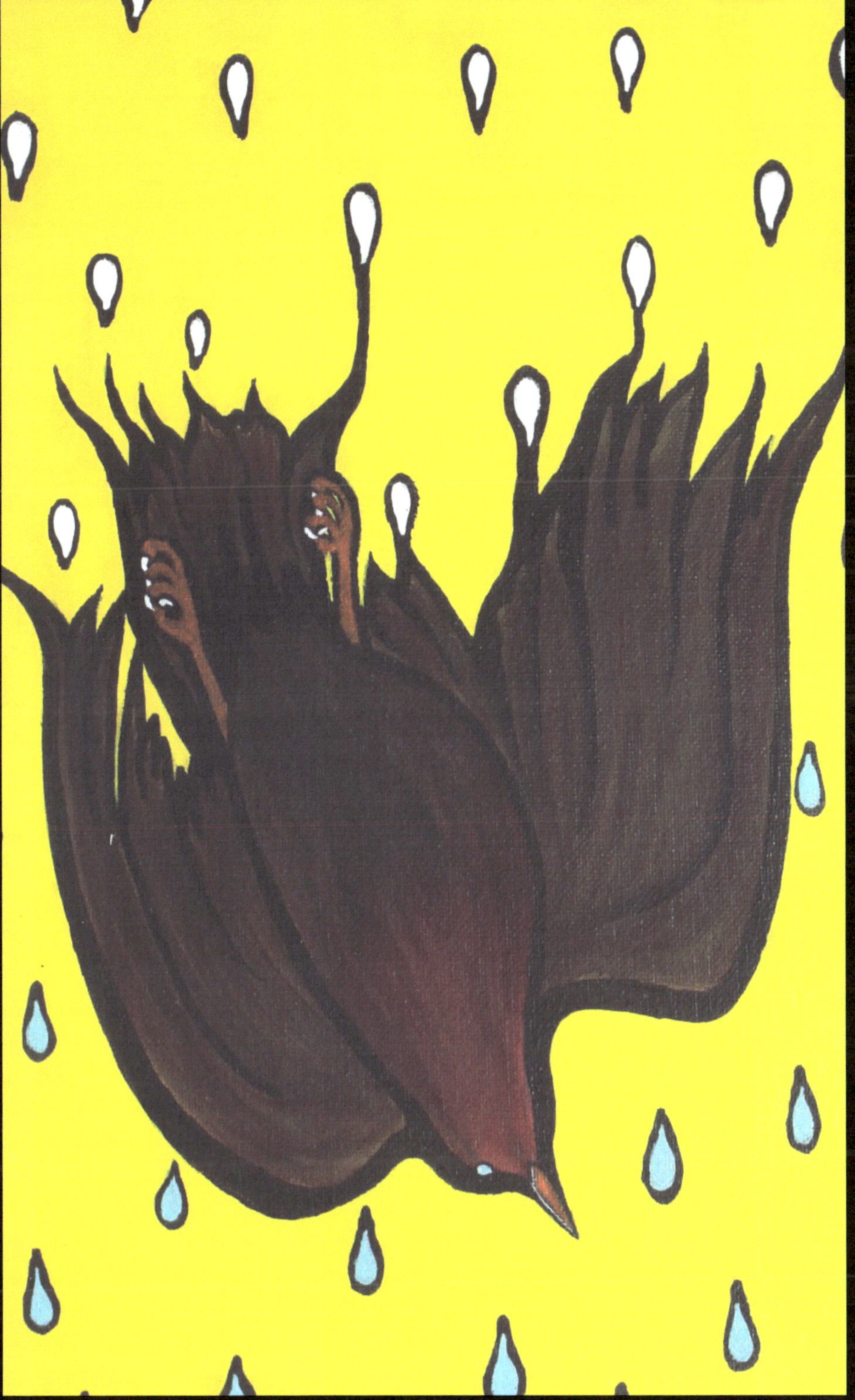

CANDLELIGHT

Candles
lit and scattered
in tribute paid
to single memory and more.

Losses
separately
invading empty spaces,
the unspoken requiem
dislodged from my heart.

I was too busy then.

Time standing
still
for the ghosts unburied
and
I run
to check the graves
are untouched
and
validation
visits again.

Too frequently
reminding me
the burden of love.

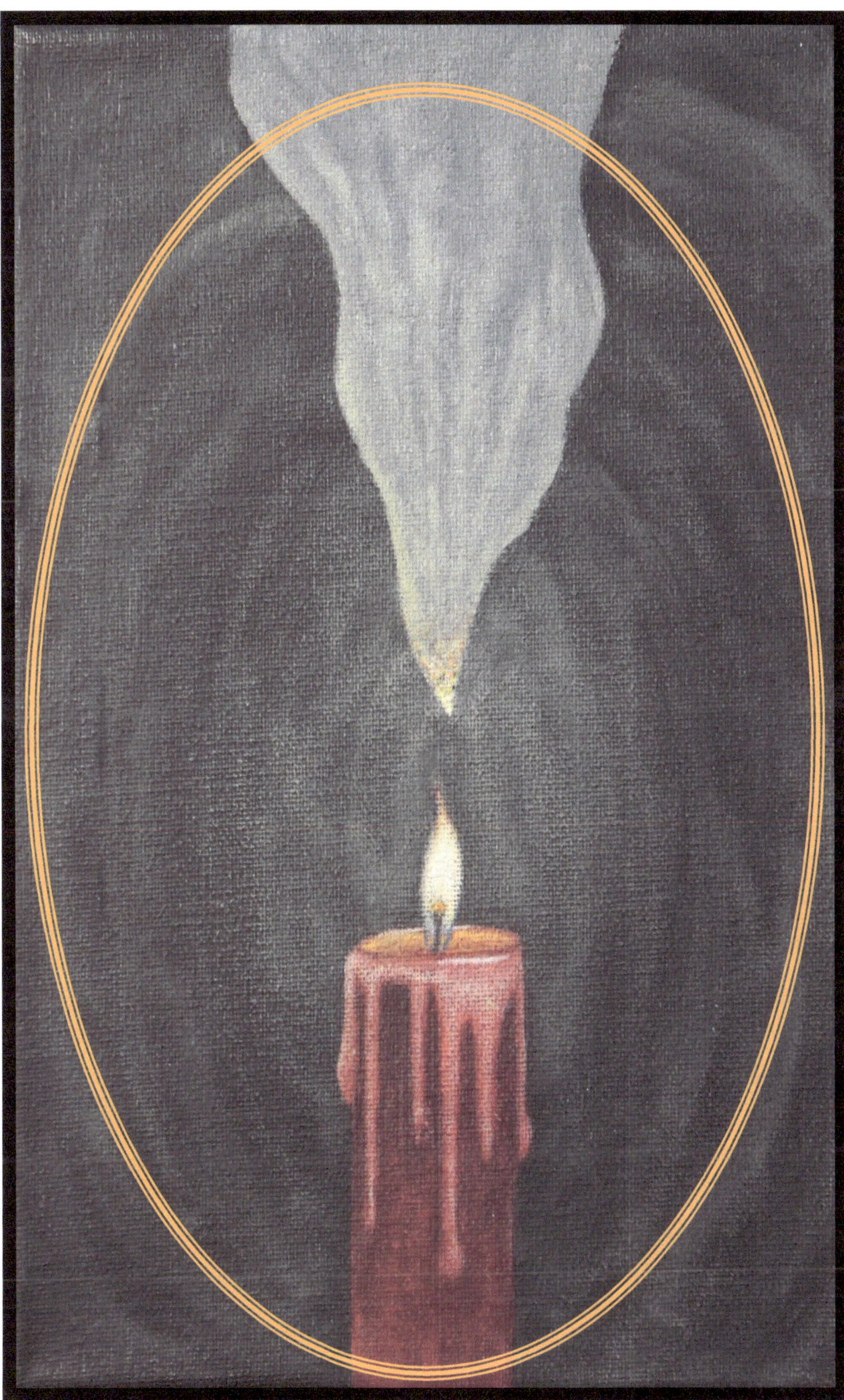

THE COLOR OF ASHES

Amber sparks
red –
lively spreading destruction

It begins.

Red burns
blue –
in its consuming battle for breath

It rages.

Blue spawns
white –
a celebratory dance,
ethereal and pure.

It lingers.

Concealed in
blackness
is
tomorrow
and
rebirth.

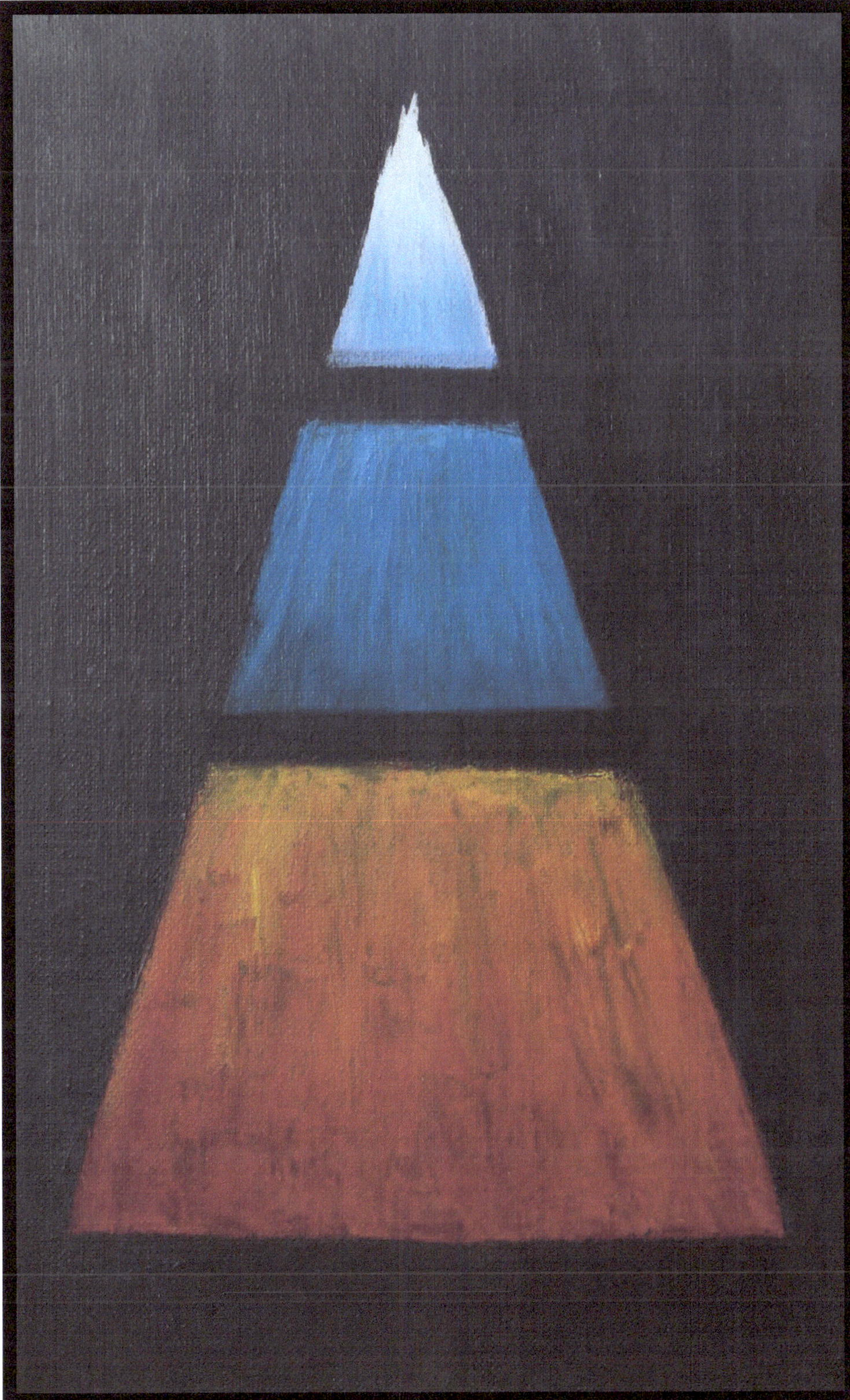

COSMIC YEARNING

Galaxies
spinning over my crib.
Calling me
"come play".
I remember

Gazing,
my eyes too small.
Reaching.
Stretching on tip-toe
could not touch the stars.
I remember

Crispness and snowflakes
embrace me.
Andromeda beckoned
from the Eastern sky.
I was yearning and no longer innocent.
I remember

Spinning wisdom
weaves the stardust.
My tapestry of dreams
unreachable.
Leaving me earthbound
and deciduous.
Halley's comet
never to return
in a lifetime.
I remember

Memories
betray my final breath.
Legacy remains
for the universe never forgets.

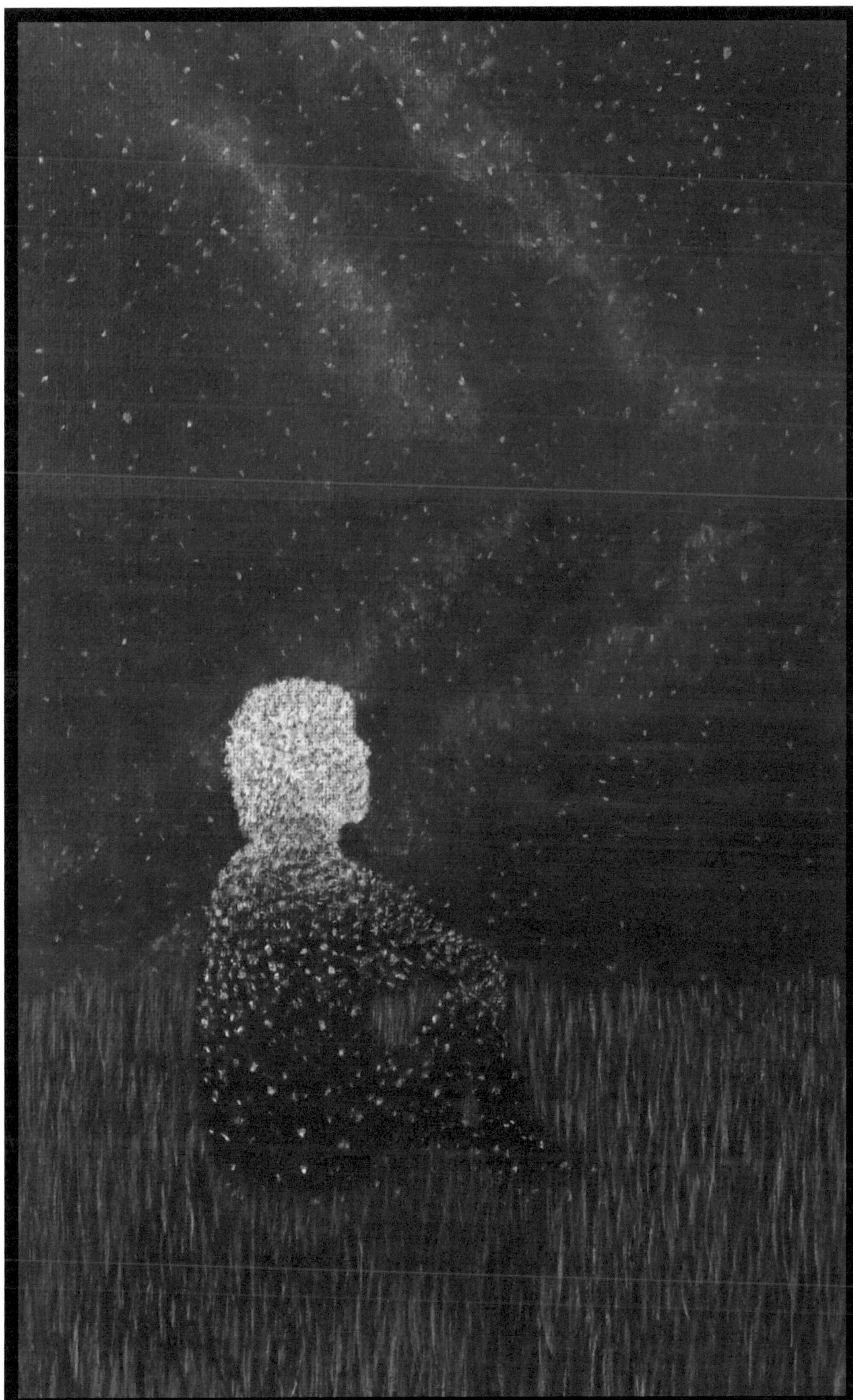

DEPTH PERCEPTION

I AM SHALLOW.

If I lived
deeply enough to understand –
the gift of awareness
would conquer my fear.

I AM SHALLOW.

If I lived
deeply in the light of unknowing,
the gift of awareness
would hold me safe from harm.

I AM SHALLOW.

If I lived deeply
and
a solitary breath
promised nothing,
the gift of awareness
would awaken in me
a magical thinking.

I AM SHALLOW.

If I lived
deeply
I would believe
it was meant to be.

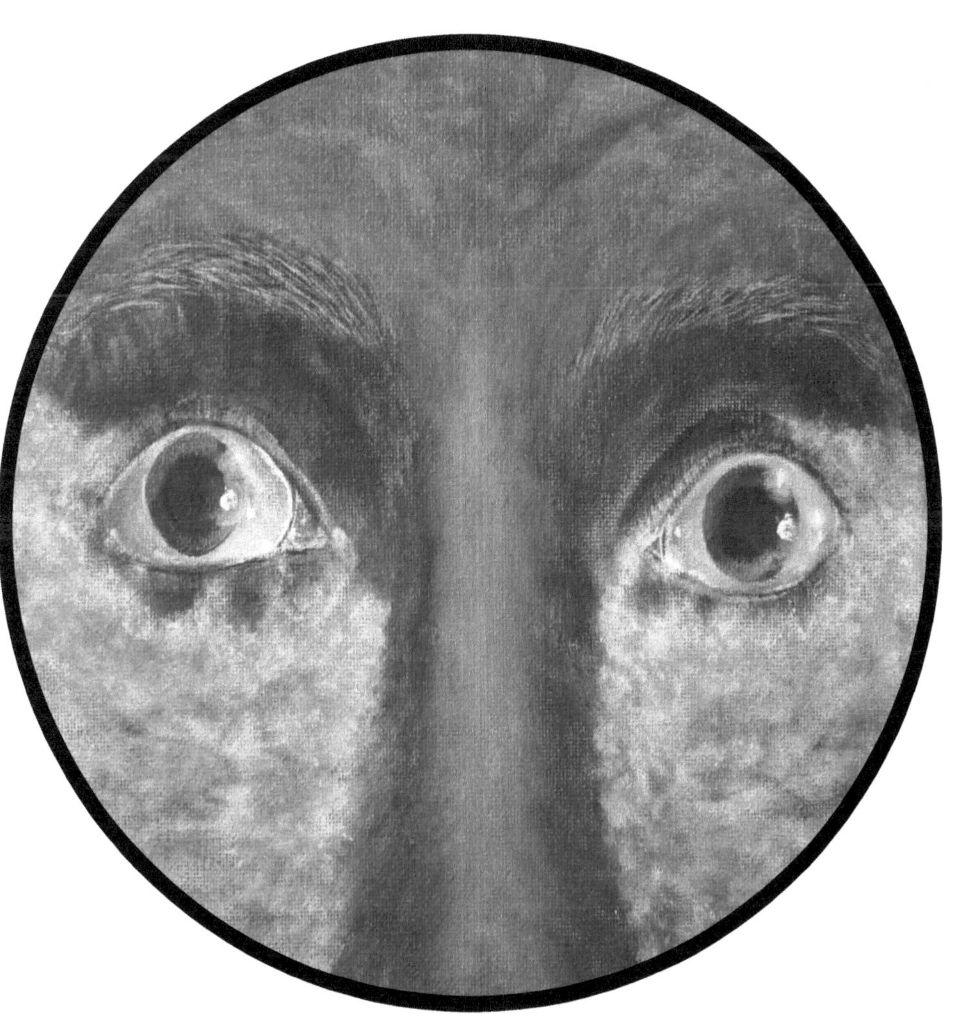

DIMINISHED MIRAGE

Colors faded.
The rainbow -
a neutral palette in my life.

Moments of differentiation
blended
into monochromatic
attempts
of living.

Truth disrobed
through the cataracts
and
aging gray matter.

Nothingness
and
silence beckon.

I was never here.

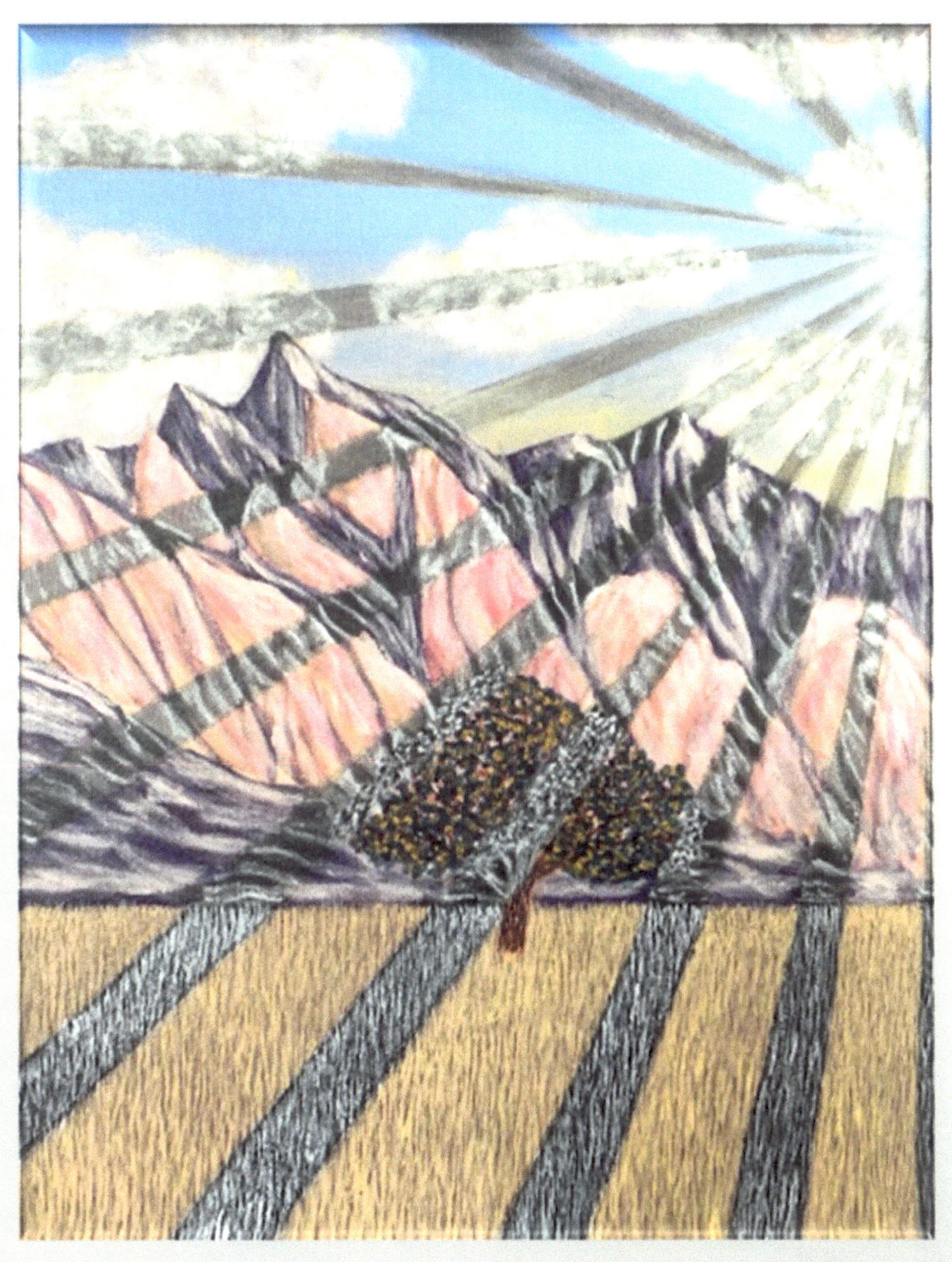

ECHOES

I hear them
long after I awaken
from
breathless dreaming.

The dead speak to me
and
I know them too well.
They are mine
as they were mine then.

Timing is a gift –
my nothing days
drift into nothing nights
and
I am joyous in the reunion.

My secret life
awakened in promised dreams.

Unafraid, I breathe out
the mundaneness of today.
We connect in
that place
between existence
and
longing.

Disruption comes
and
I must leave
this perfect place.
Their echoes keeping me company
on this solitary journey

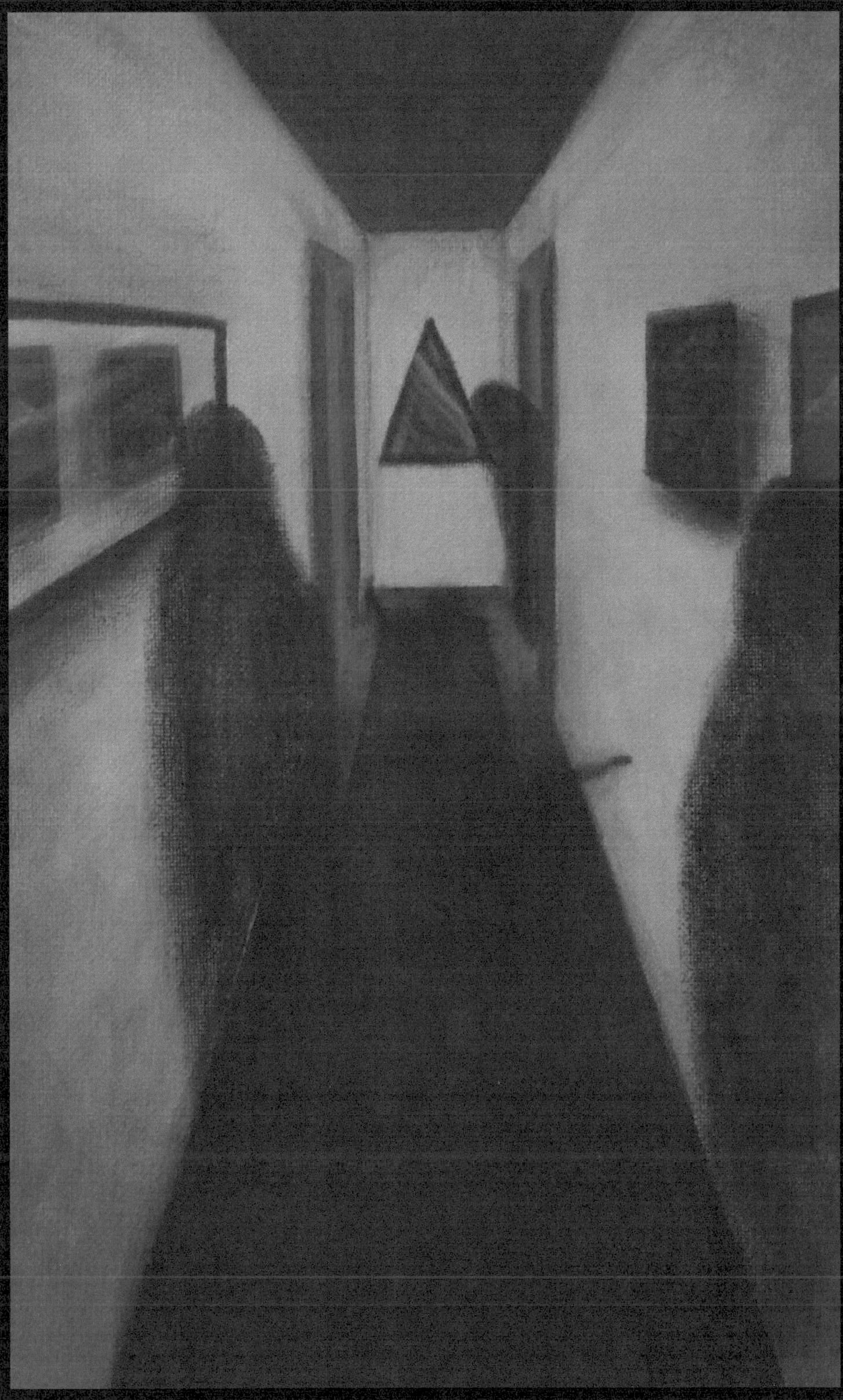

EMPATH'S DENIAL

Klingon mind-meld
is real.
It happens between
him and me.
Unification of two disparate souls
on
an uneven playing field.

Life is just that way.

Constant depletion and replenishment
in the dying embers
of a newlywed's dreams –
too long ago.

I will play my part
in this complicit entanglement
of contracted nuptials –
until desire abates
and
breath no longer visits.

Life is just that way.

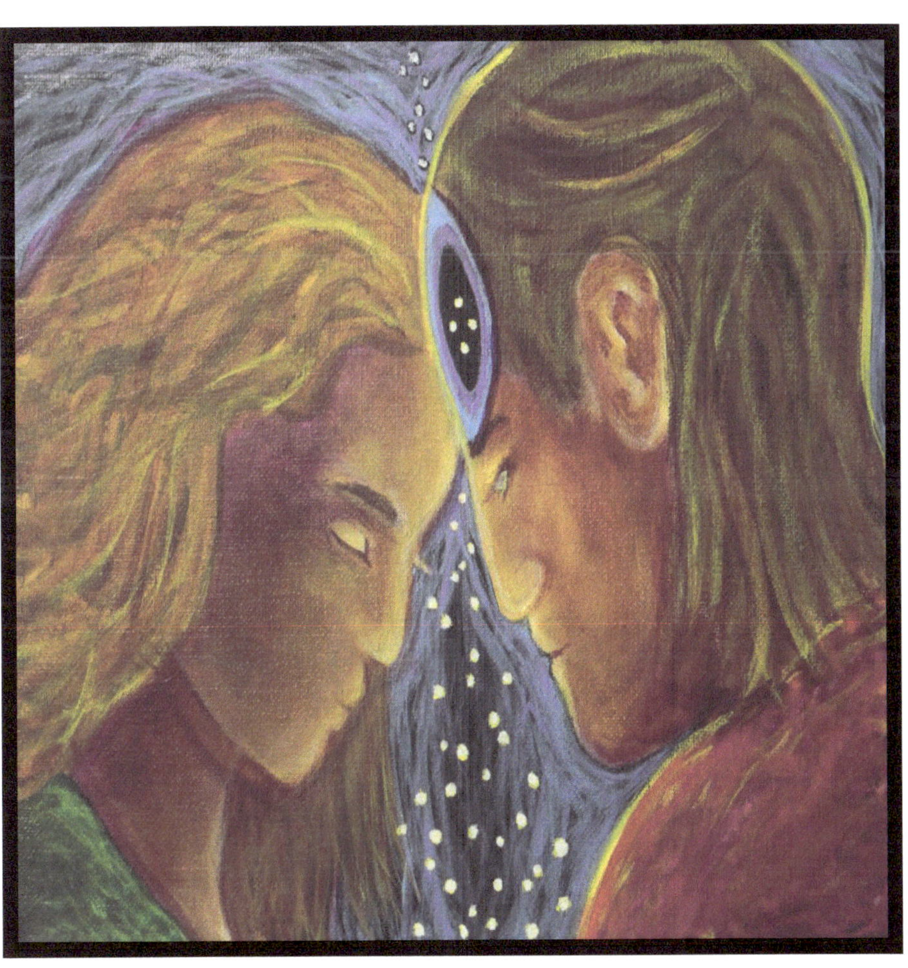

GAZING

My door frame
frames a door frame
through which the laced curtain
frames a window.

The sunlight filters through
and greets the solitary plant,
so purposefully centered on the sill.

My gaze is interrupted
by the age old glass-
worn and crackled by time
and
my unwillingness to wash it.

He lays in the next room
mostly alive
and
his breathing
heavily burdened by life choices.

I lay in my bed
under the bedclothes
of
yellow and powder-blue quilts
without
a care in the world.

I don't know why
I am content.
But I am.

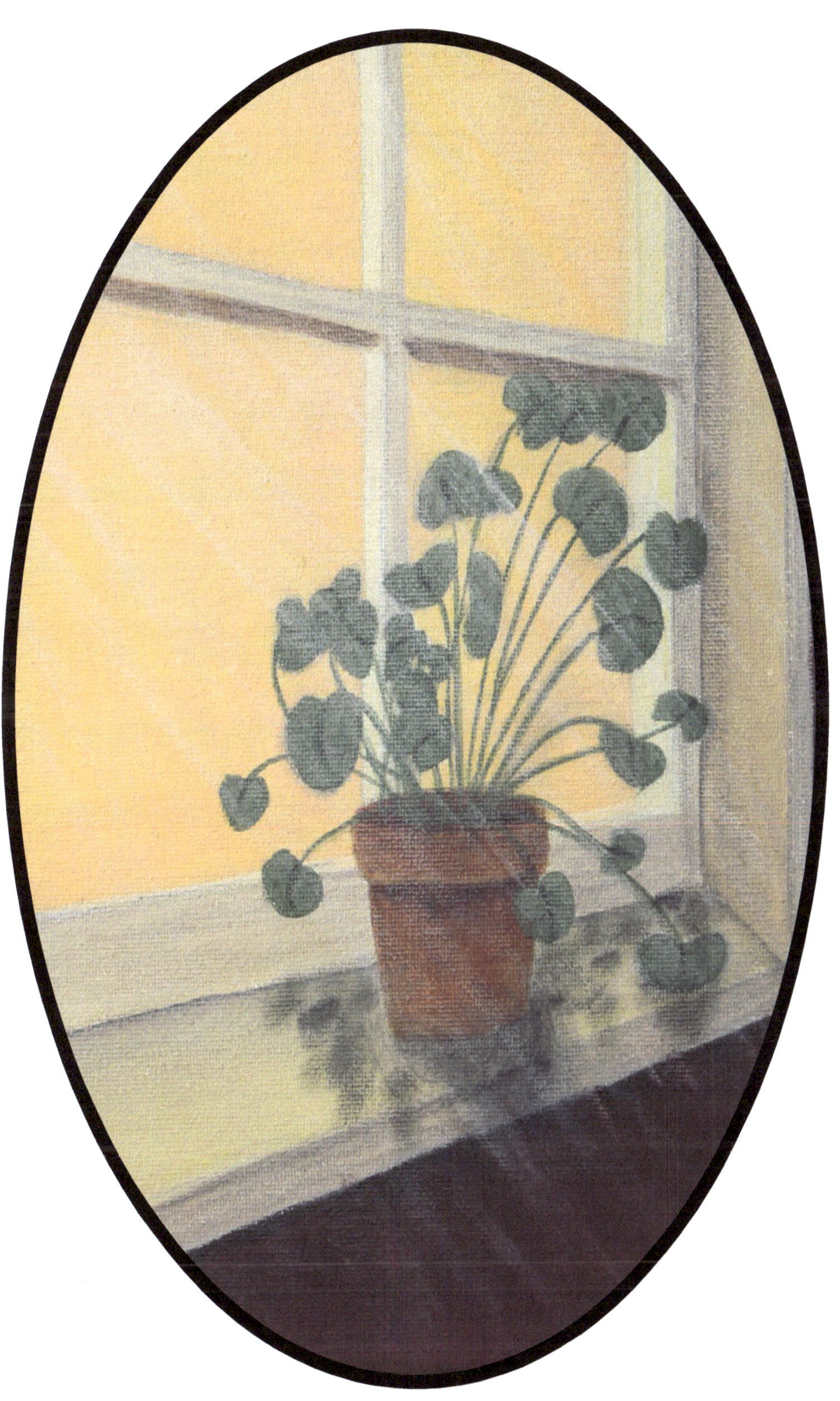

HOMESICK

Dreams bleeding
stain the pages
of my memory.

Red fog
beckoning
and
small footprints
obscured.

Nothing to comfort
wishes of
the child within.

Home and
the raven
whispers
"Nevermore."

Change
is the chainsaw
severing the arteries
of
what used to be.

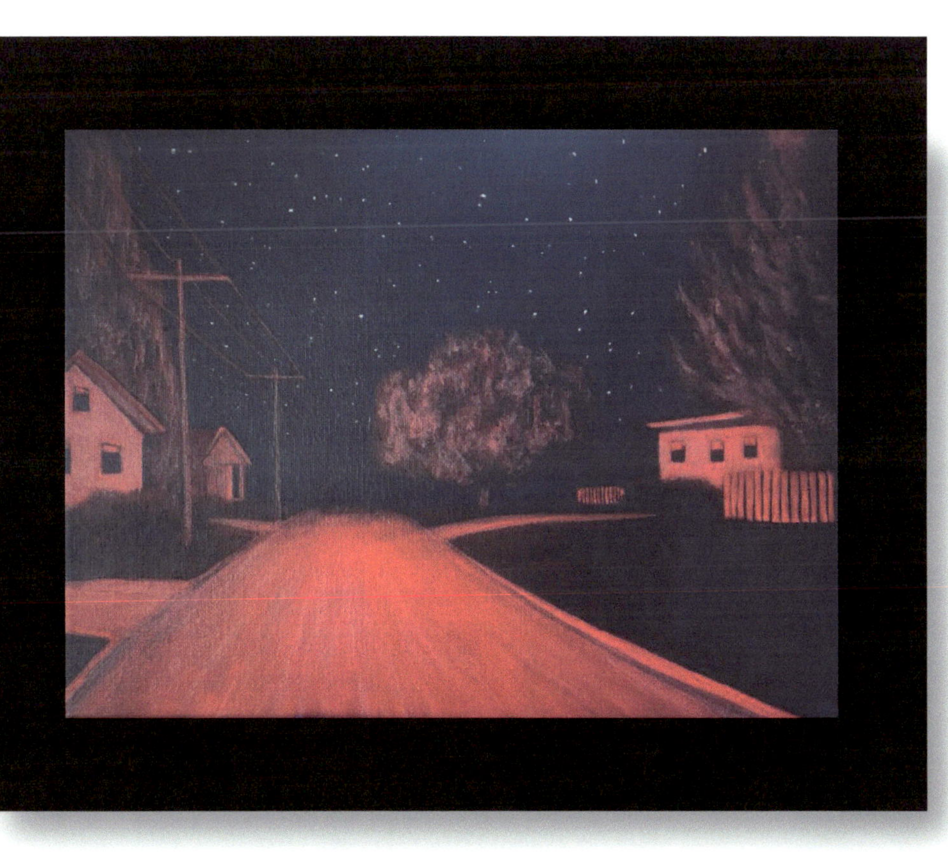

IMPERMANENCE

Life and death
are the same.
Portals -
of
temporary existence.
No need for hype.

The soul's reentry
comes full circle –
and
darkness awaits sweet reunion.

Evolution
masks wasted celebrations.
Emotional debris
takes root
in promises
kept or forgotten.

Atoms bursting
from decaying dreams.
Time is an illusion
and
nothing matters.

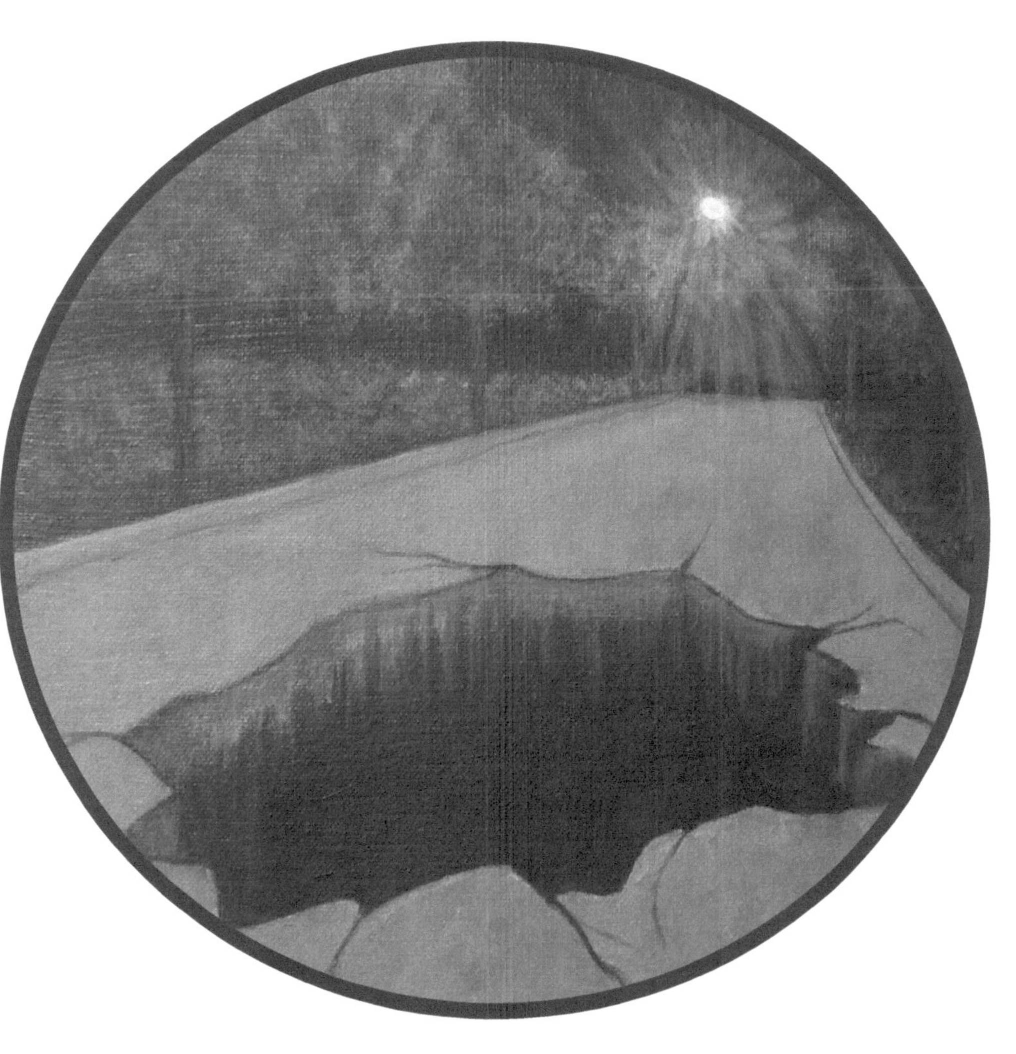

INFINITY

A different forest
of technicolor dreams,

And I witnessed -
Forever

Vaguely familiar
as I felt earth
beneath
my carefree stride

And I witnessed -
Forever

Pausing -
to gaze at forms,
seeking
respite under starlit canopy.

And I witnessed –
Forever

Shapes
and
textures
reminiscent of my
long ago.
Do not awaken me.

I cannot breathe

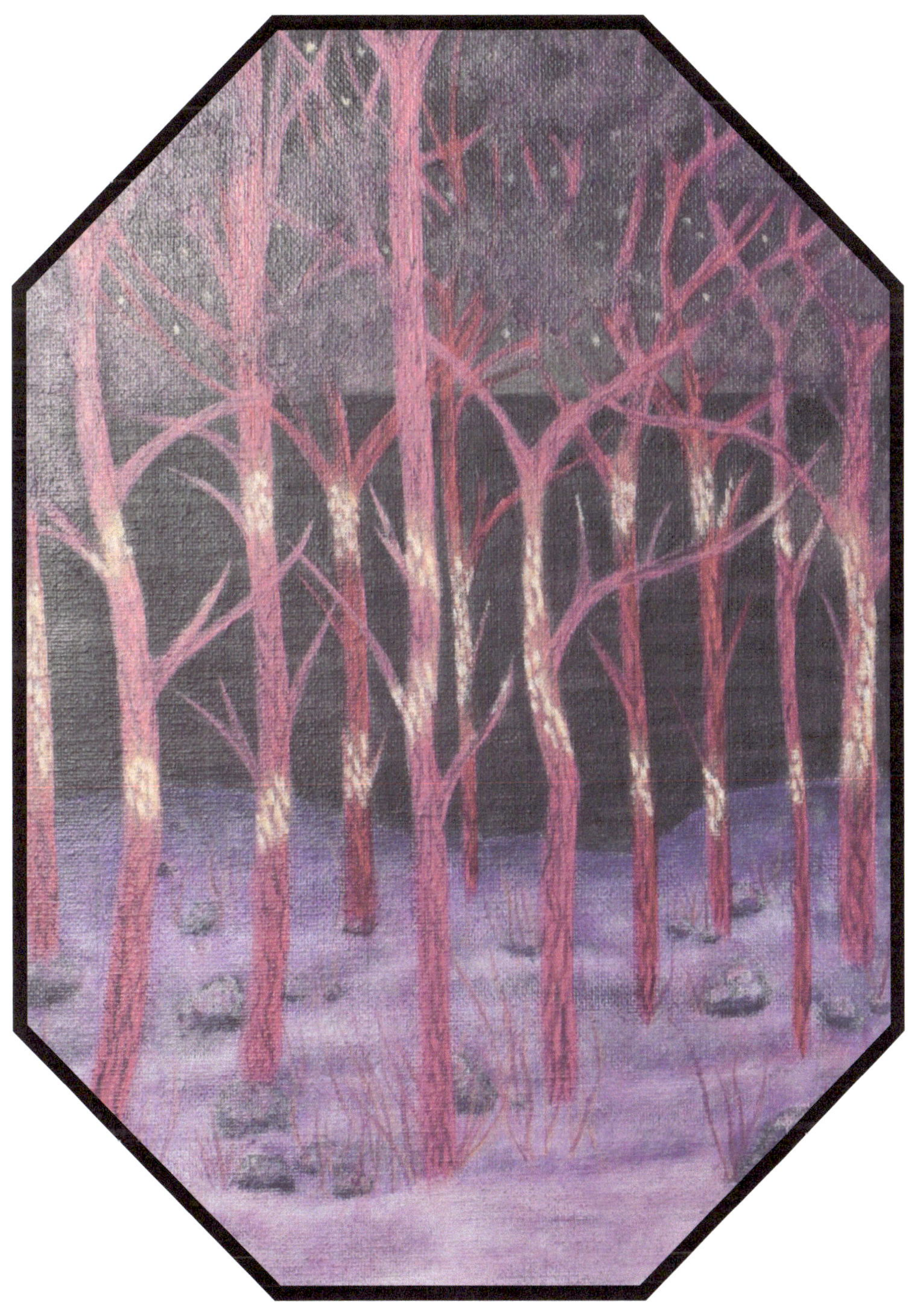

LANDSCAPE

Am I
the jagged and scarred
canyon walls -
- carved by the
purveyor of time?

Am I
the whitecaps -
raging above the
calmness of still waters;
prisoner of natural forces
I cannot comprehend?

Am I
the ebb and flow
of granite beings –
listless dragons preserved
for rebirth?

Am I
green and colours
of deception –
under and over,
beckoning an awareness
and discovery of purpose?

Am I
in galaxies far beyond
where the senses
cannot interpret my truth?

Revelation cometh.

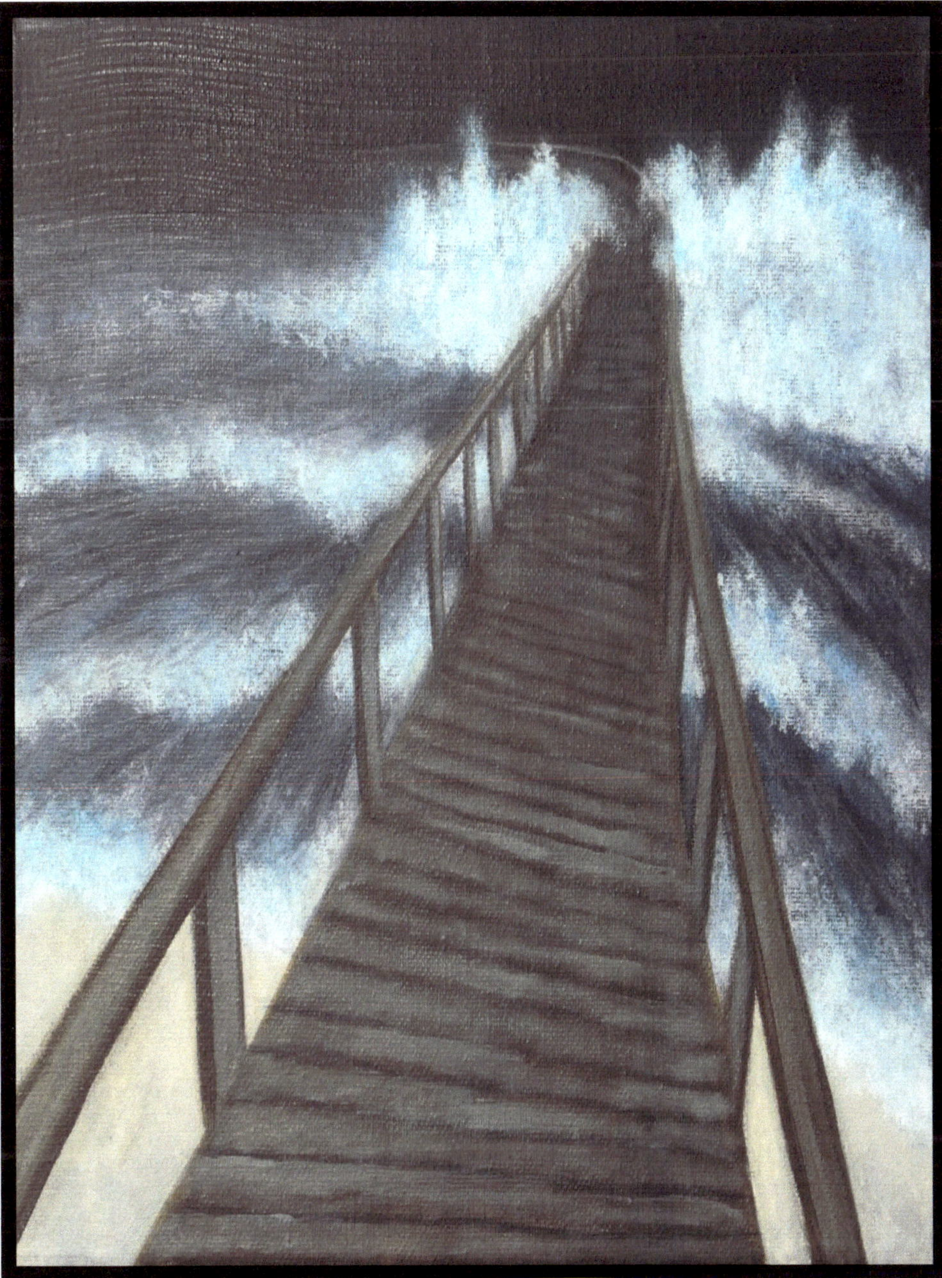

LIVE LIKE SOMEONE

LEFT THE GATE OPEN

Gates and doors,
thresholds and portals
invite the curious
and
desperate souls –
a quick
or
delayed moment of decision.

Movement is guaranteed
to disrupt any plans of sameness.
The present is past
or future.
Nothing lost,
except in hesitation.

Gatekeepers of life's dimensions
lining up in their soldier-esque formations
keeping time sacred.
For the reveal lies in the heart
and
mind of the pilgrim.

Freedom is
redefined
in the letting go.

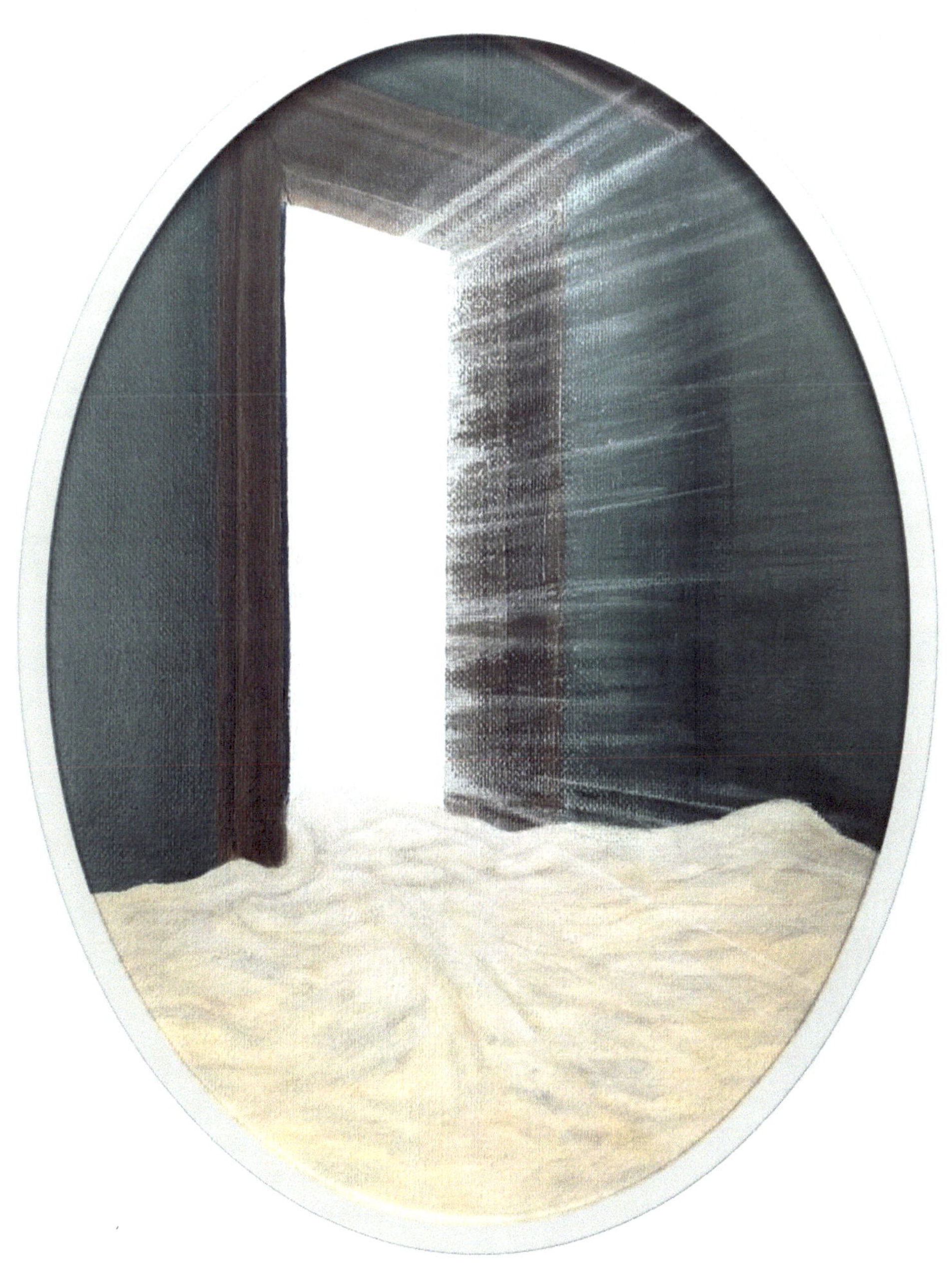

LOVE BY DROWNING

Gasping for love.
I tread the
rip tide that is you.
Moonlight in deceitful shimmer
upon the tide
too deep
and
far from shore.

Holding my breath
I go under -
endlessly aware
of light bubbling sky ward.

Sinking until
I don't care anymore
and
float.

Beautiful surrender
releasing broken promises
upon the waves.

Flowing and lovely,
deep water
embraces.
Invulnerable.
Safe in the murky
sediment.

My voice
lapping against the shore.
Fading footprints
echoing
farewell.

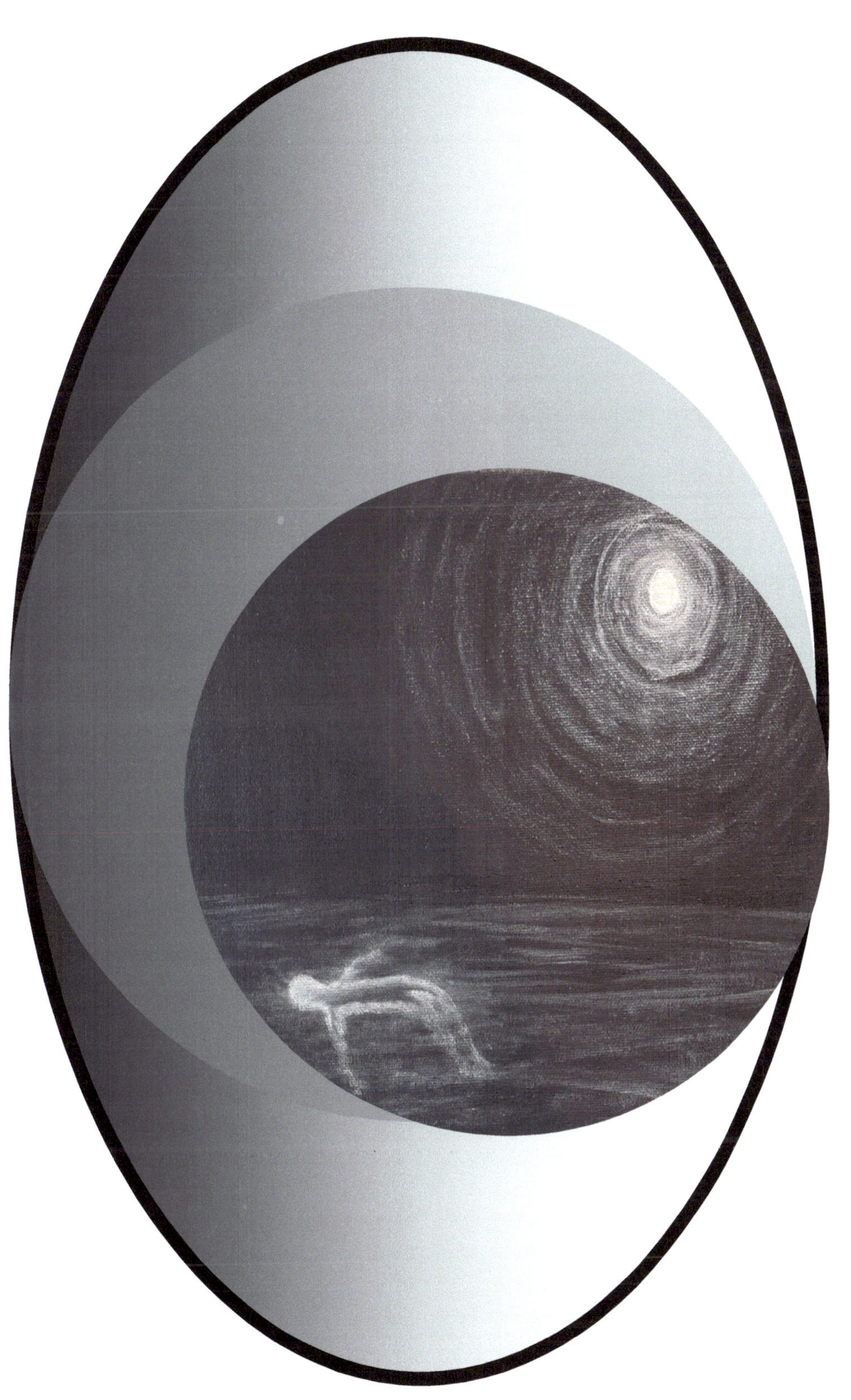

ME, UNDEAD

She is elegant.
Death –
mistily embracing
my waiting crypt.

Remains
so carefully preserved
will in time
disfigure.
Tender roots will
desperately claw
the rotting soil.

And transformation begins
as promised
and
faith has no cause
to claim the victory, for I was interrupted
in this journey.

Predestined traveler
and
innocent of fate
my path is lighted in
stardust
where I began.

Reunion
when I am the
dust beneath your feet.

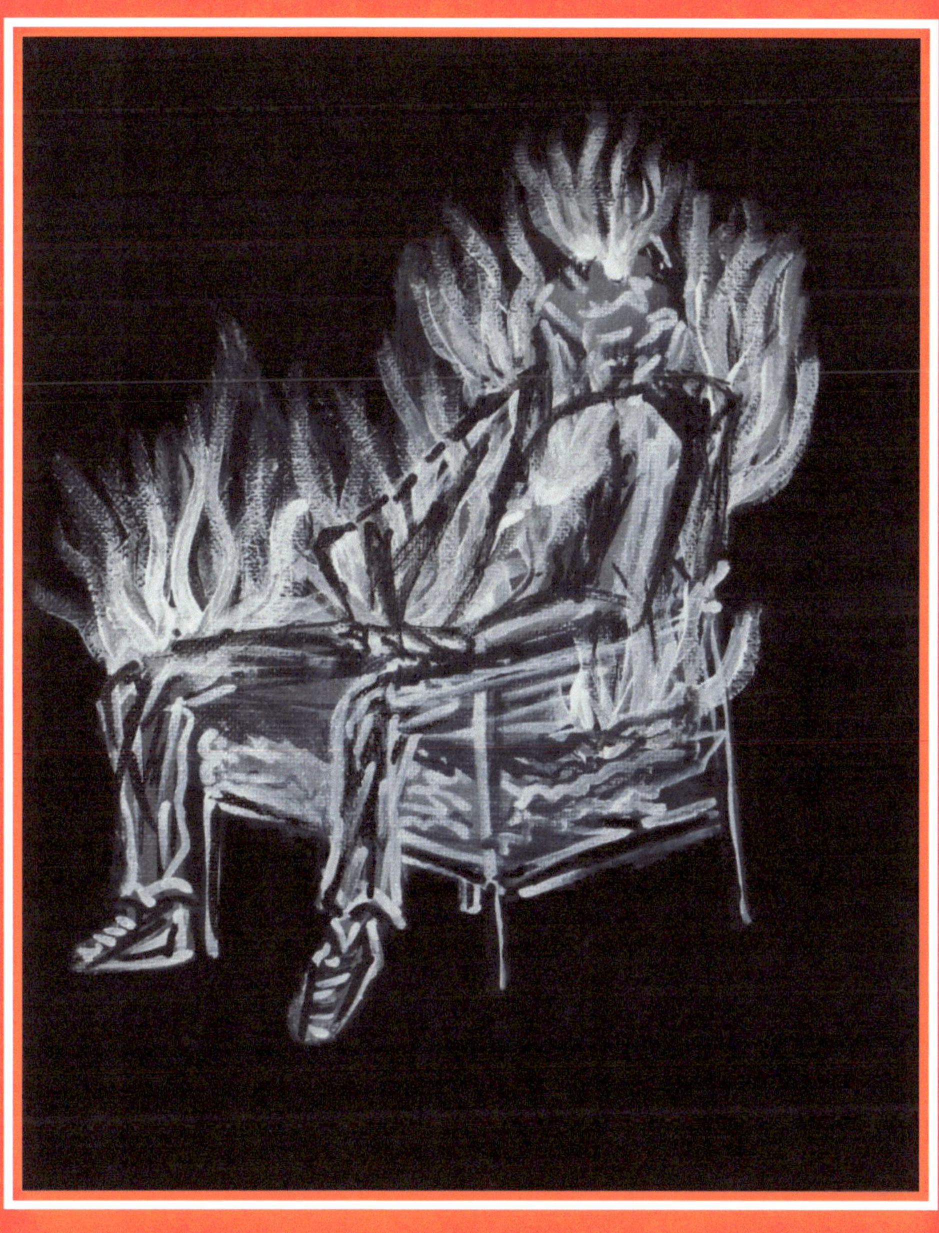

PETRIFIED

I was
the hopeful
seedling
on the breeze.

Within me –
promise
of a tree.
Rooted in shifting sands.

Waiting, yearning.
Seasons corresponding
with each fallen leaf
and
bud.

Gifting shade
to no one and
branches stretched –
untouched.

Gnarled and twisted,
graceful silhouette –
the desert sustaining
and unforgiving.
Perfection.
Reflection of an imperfect
god.

Purpose revealed –
Mirrored in the eternal oasis
of my dreams.

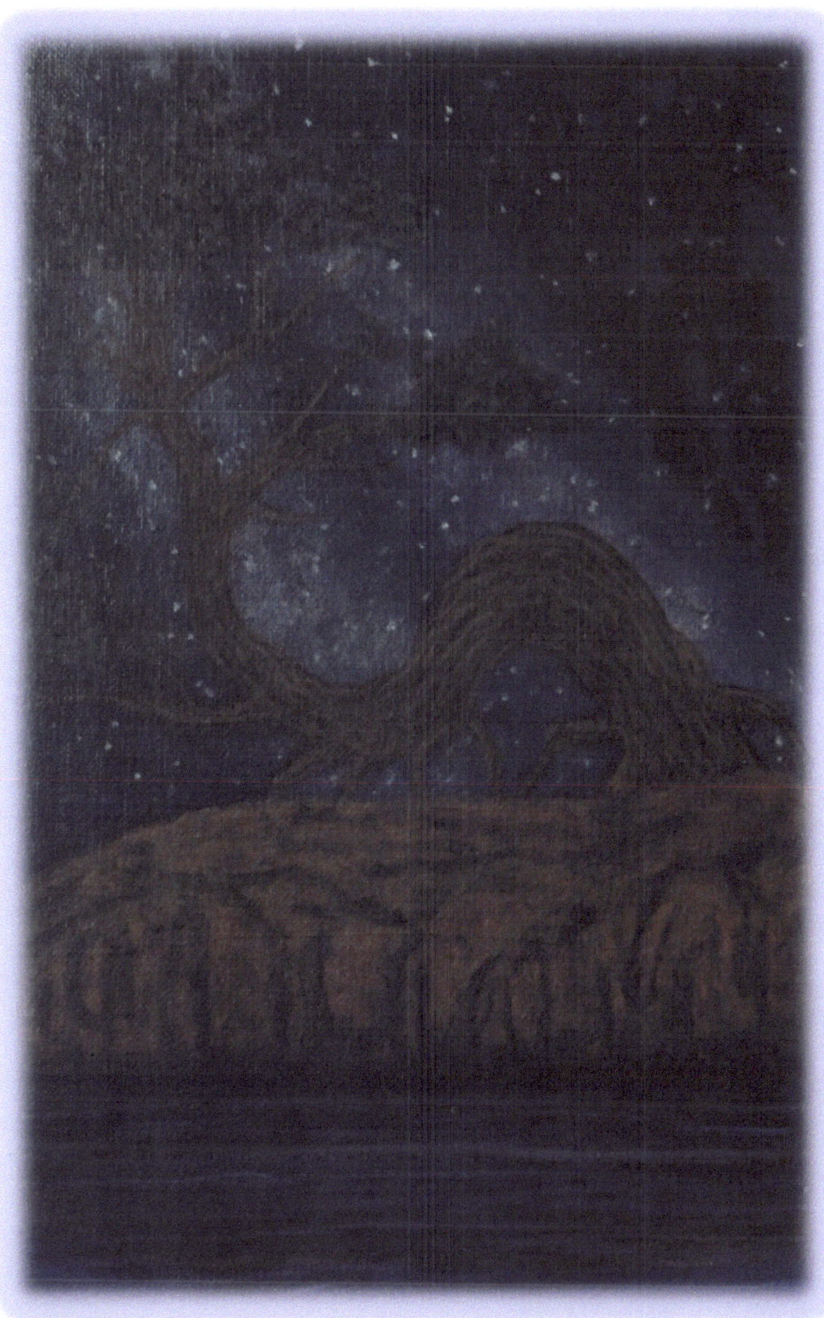

PURPLENESS

Not quite sanguine
the brush dips blue
adding sadness
to the depth
where I do not recover.

The color is heavy.
Burden is the culmination
of too much trying.

Feeling my life
through the endless
colors
splatters the pristineness
of the canvas
laden with cobwebs.

Falling upward –
the rainbow embraces
and the sun is warm.
Reminding me
to put the paint box away.

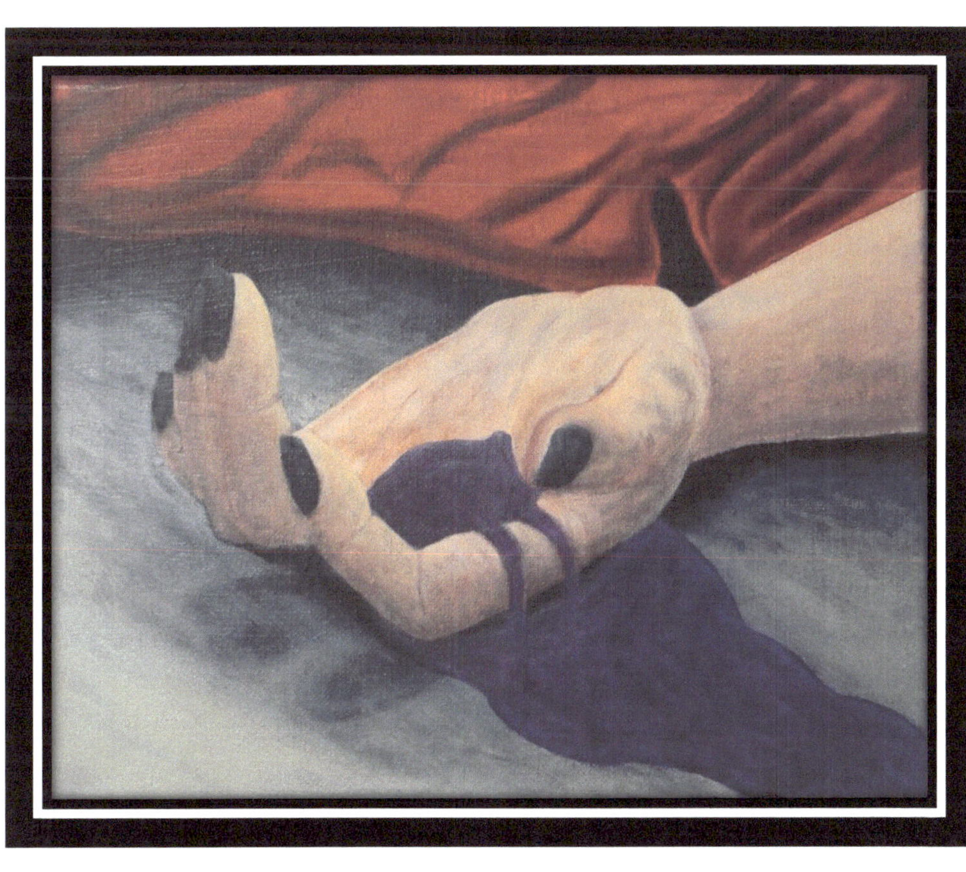

RELEASE

Release comes
and the path
now laden
and
heavy in fog.

My burden to carry.

Release comes
and my steadfastness
fractured –
until
my breath is replenished.
and
I
am
who I am.

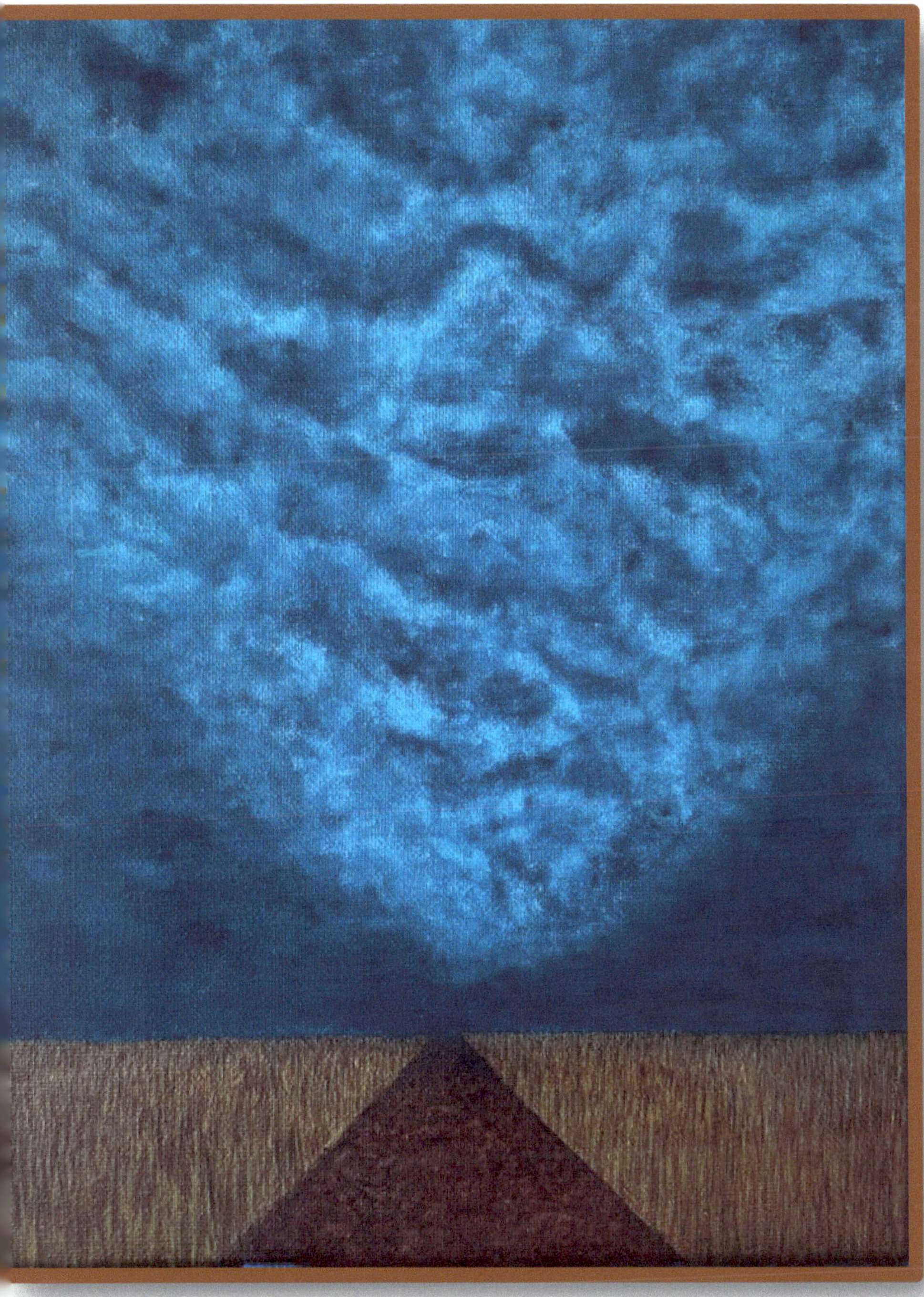

THE MASQUERADE

Death has come
to visit
and
try me on for size.

Each corner I am turning
I look straight into
the eyes
of one most haunting.

And yet –
familiar.

The parts of me
I gave away
are back
and
so ill-fitting
belonging to another me.

So long away
I can't remember.
Let me slumber
and
awaken where the fog
denies
the hopeful heart.

Illustrator Interview
by Laura Kester Duerrwaechter

Why did you decide to collaborate on this book?

After reading a few poems and having multiple conversations, it became clear to me that not only were our artistic styles similar, but we ourselves were very similar down to a spiritual level. We look at the universe in a like-minded fashion, and I figured it would be fascinating to interpret your words with my images.

What poems draw you in?

I am often drawn to poems that concern rather dark or macabre concepts, and poetry that expresses universal beauty; whether like your poem 'Purple-ness," which expresses great sadness, or like "Cosmic Yearning", which relays the desire to know more, and to be more in-tune with our own spiritually and connectedness to everything around us.

Explain your relationship with sacred geometry and why the triangle is central to several of your original paintings for this book.

I find sacred geometry interesting as it involves naturally repeating patterns. The same patterns, tessellations and flows are found throughout not just nature, but the universe as well. The veins in our body mimic branches of a tree which in turn mimic the mycelium network connecting all the surrounding plant life. And this pattern is seen in how celestial bodies are woven together. To understand natural patterns and progressions is to receive a better understanding of just how interconnected everything really is. Triangles I find fascinating, as they are the strongest naturally occurring shape and have been a very important architectural and symbolic shape through all cultures since the dawn of man.

Are you a painter/lyricist or other way around? Does one creative process feed off the other? Balance it?

I simply consider myself a creator. All arts I practice feed off of another. I prefer to paint the beauty I see in life. I enjoy capturing the color of foliage, the shapes of flowers and fungi, the energy and soul of animals and humans. I can tell infinitely many stories whether hopeful or sad, and I can do it through capturing the sempiternal beauty of the natural world.

I prefer to write dark lyrics as I find writing is a way more descriptive way for me to capture the complex array of negative emotions such as fear, sadness, hopelessness, and trauma. As someone who practices vocals daily as well, I find awe in the wide range of vocal sounds that can be used to express all these emotions. How a simple pitch change can take a verse from apathetic to agony. I sing the entire time I paint. I feed off the energy from the music and transfer it into whatever I am painting. The music helps me find and keep rhythm in my work. Sixteen notes become quickly growing individual grasses and leaves. Long soulful crones become flowing strands of hair and cascading shade changes. Balance is found in the mixture of composure and chaos. All art must contain this balance.

The lyrics you write are dark. What is your message?

My message I suppose would be sharing words that can be hard to say or talk about. Expressing existential sadness or talking about addiction and trauma is not fun. And it's not something that is usually comfortable to talk about. Most of the time, these intense feelings and experiences get pushed under the rug so to say, and they only build pressure over time. I aim to be a voice that expresses these emotions in a very poignant and realistic manner. I want my lyrics to remind people that it's okay to be not be okay. And there is always a path forward that you can carve yourself. There can be no light without the presence of darkness; just as there can be no success without repeated failures. Trust in your resolve, trust the process, and focus on the positive.

You have obviously studied/observed The Masters. Do you draw inspiration from anyone in particular?

I would not say that I draw inspiration from anyone in particular content-wise, as my paintings are the stories of my soul. However, I do pull a small amount of inspiration style-wise from painters such as Gustav Klimt and Maxfield Parrish, and layout-wise from old Baroque paintings. I balance fine detail with more surreal aspects. I try to create fever-dreamesque paintings that you don't simply look at; you experience. I aspire for viewers to take their time and pull in every piece of detail I've included in my work. Every time someone looks at a piece of mine, I want them to notice something new.

You seem to thrive on gallery presentations with your paintings. The originals I have seen are strong and the story line can be easily interpreted. Have you considered murals?

I thrive on gallery settings as they offer a confined space to display multiple stories and multiple variations on my style. I have considered doing murals before, however have decided that I prefer the accessibility of using canvas. My fine detailed style I feel is better captured on the smooth even surface of a canvas wrapped frame. Working outdoors presents a multitude of new options and subject matter. Still though, I am perfectly content covering people's interior walls with my canvas work.

You are equally comfortable with realism, fantasy and whimsy. Is there a thread of commonality as far as technique? What is your process? How do you choose subject matter?

I use the same acrylic layering techniques through all the styles I paint. Whether painting multiple layers and colors of hair, painting large ombre' areas on more surrealist style pieces, my techniques for blending and layering stay the same. I am a huge fan of different dry brushing techniques, and creating ways to glaze different colors. Building up colors and blending the colors both ways to create smooth finishes and transitions in the colors are very important in every style I paint.

I choose my subject matter to tell a story or represent certain emotions or situations. I paint women in positions of strength, showing resilience, intuition, kindness, and forgiveness. I pair these figures with animals I feel capture certain feelings. I use forest animals such as foxes and ravens to represent the chaos, unpredictability, and harsh reality of life. While using smaller animals such as frogs, mice, and rabbits to represent the more innocent and vulnerable emotions of life. The juxtaposition of the two different animal types creates a peace and erases any predatory/prey aspect between the animals. This represents the coming to peace with, understanding, and control of one's inner emotions and strife. Blending and consciously considering the highs and lows of life creates a peaceful neutral mindset where one can look at situations through more than just one lens.

How do you know when you have finished a painting?

Deciding when a painting is finished is always a difficult decision. It ultimately comes down to when I decide I'm simply nitpicking features of a painting that are perfectly fine as is. When I feel I could potentially create negative progress, is when I put down the brush.

Https://www.n11fineart.com/

Instagram: @november11_acrylics

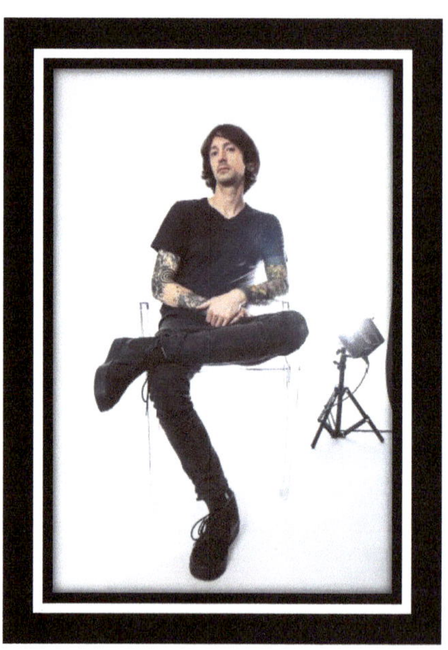

Author Biography

Laura Kester Duerrwaechter is an indie author known for her diverse perspectives. She has published collections of poetry and short stories, memoirs, speculative fiction, and her first illustrated children's book series is due out in 2025.

She is daring and unafraid to share thought provoking words that sometimes linger in uncomfortable places. She is currently living in the Florida Panhandle where she mentors other creatives and is an active Patron of the Arts and community volunteer.

She is a member of The Horror Writers Association and occasional contributor to Space and Time Magazine. The University of Arizona Poetry Center has a complete collection of her works from 2017 through 2025. Other designated libraries include Fairview High School, Boulder, CO, Northwest Florida State College (Niceville campus), and several Little Free Libraries.

Her books can be found on Amazon.com.

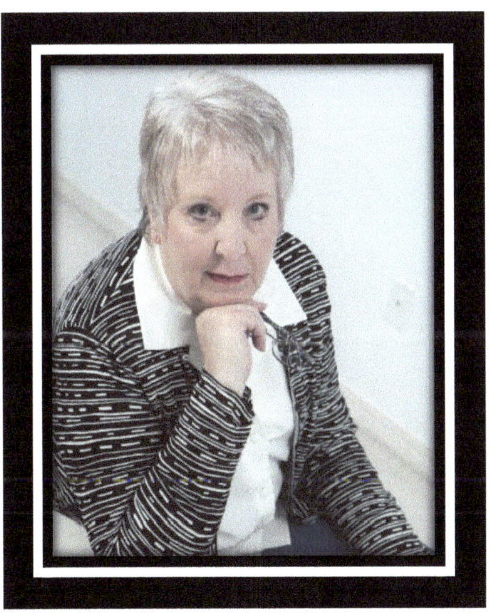

www.ingramcontent.com/pod-product-compliance
Lightning Source LLC
LaVergne TN
LVHW052300100826
845147LV00001B/96

* 9 7 8 1 9 5 9 0 4 8 3 2 9 *